EXTRAORDINARY CLAIMS
REQUIRE EXTRAORDINARY EVIDENCE.

—CARL SAGAN

EVIDENCE

IDENTIFICATION No. EKJR812

DATE OF COLLECTION: ___ / ___ / ___   TIME OF COLLECTION: _____ □ AM □ PM

MODE OF COLLECTION: □ OBSERVED □ OVERHEARD □ OTHER _____

LOCATION: _____

TYPE OF EVIDENCE: □ PHYSICAL □ CIRCUMSTANTIAL □ HEARSAY □ OTHER

DESCRIPTION: _____

CONCLUSION: _____

. . . AND THE WORLD IS BASICALLY GOOD.

□ CLEAR AND COMPELLING EVIDENCE   □ REASONABLE DOUBT

(AFFIX OR SKETCH EVIDENCE HERE)

EXHIBITS

1(a). _____

1(b). _____

EXHIBITS

1(c). _____

_____

_____

_____

_____

_____

_____

_____

_____

_____

1(d). _____

_____

_____

_____

_____

_____

_____

EXHIBITS

1(e). _____

_____

_____

_____

_____

_____

_____

_____

_____

1(f). _____

_____

_____

_____

_____

_____

_____

_____

_____

EVIDENCE

IDENTIFICATION No. EKJR813

DATE OF COLLECTION: ___ / ___ / ___

TIME OF COLLECTION: _____
- ☐ AM
- ☐ PM

MODE OF COLLECTION: ☐ OBSERVED ☐ OVERHEARD ☐ OTHER _____

LOCATION: _____

TYPE OF EVIDENCE: ☐ PHYSICAL ☐ CIRCUMSTANTIAL ☐ HEARSAY ☐ OTHER

DESCRIPTION: _____
_____
_____
_____
_____
_____
_____
_____
_____

CONCLUSION: _____
_____
_____
_____
_____ . . . AND THE WORLD IS BASICALLY GOOD.

☐ CLEAR AND COMPELLING EVIDENCE   ☐ REASONABLE DOUBT

(AFFIX OR SKETCH EVIDENCE HERE)

I AM DEEPLY IMPRESSED WITH THE DESIGNER OF THE UNIVERSE; I AM CONFIDENT
I COULDN'T HAVE DONE ANYWHERE NEAR SUCH A GOOD JOB. —BUCKMINSTER FULLER

EXHIBITS

2(a).

2(b).

EXHIBITS

2(c).

2(d).

EXHIBITS

2(e). _____

_____

_____

_____

_____

_____

_____

_____

2(f). _____

_____

_____

_____

_____

_____

_____

EVIDENCE

IDENTIFICATION No. EKJR814

DATE OF COLLECTION: _____ / _____ / _____   TIME OF COLLECTION: _____ □ AM □ PM

MODE OF COLLECTION: □ OBSERVED □ OVERHEARD □ OTHER _____

LOCATION: _____

TYPE OF EVIDENCE: □ PHYSICAL □ CIRCUMSTANTIAL □ HEARSAY □ OTHER

DESCRIPTION: _____
_____
_____
_____
_____
_____
_____
_____
_____
_____
_____
_____

CONCLUSION: _____
_____
_____
_____
_____
_____
. . . AND THE WORLD IS BASICALLY GOOD.

□ CLEAR AND COMPELLING EVIDENCE   □ REASONABLE DOUBT

(AFFIX OR SKETCH EVIDENCE HERE)

EVERYWHERE IN THE WORLD, YOU FIND GOOD THINGS. —JEAN RENO

EXHIBITS

3(a). _____

3(b). _____

EXHIBITS

3(c).

3(d).

EXHIBITS

3(e).

3(f).

EVIDENCE

IDENTIFICATION No. EKJR815

DATE OF COLLECTION: ___ / ___ / ___   TIME OF COLLECTION: _____ □ AM □ PM

MODE OF COLLECTION: □ OBSERVED   □ OVERHEARD   □ OTHER _____

LOCATION: _____

TYPE OF EVIDENCE: □ PHYSICAL   □ CIRCUMSTANTIAL   □ HEARSAY   □ OTHER

DESCRIPTION: _____

_____

_____

_____

_____

_____

_____

✀

_____

_____

CONCLUSION: _____

_____

_____

_____

_____ . . . AND THE WORLD IS BASICALLY GOOD.

□ CLEAR AND COMPELLING EVIDENCE   □ REASONABLE DOUBT

(AFFIX OR SKETCH EVIDENCE HERE)

MAN IS NOT MADE FOR DEFEAT. —ERNEST HEMINGWAY

EXHIBITS

4(a). _____

_____

_____

_____

_____

_____

_____

_____

_____

_____

4(b). _____

_____

_____

_____

_____

_____

_____

_____

_____

_____

EXHIBITS

4(c). _____

4(d). _____

EXHIBITS

4(e). _____

_____

_____

_____

_____

_____

_____

_____

_____

4(f). _____

_____

_____

_____

_____

_____

_____

_____

EVIDENCE

IDENTIFICATION No. EKJR816

DATE OF COLLECTION: ___ / ___ / ___

TIME OF COLLECTION: _____
☐ AM
☐ PM

MODE OF COLLECTION: ☐ OBSERVED ☐ OVERHEARD ☐ OTHER

LOCATION: _____

TYPE OF EVIDENCE: ☐ PHYSICAL ☐ CIRCUMSTANTIAL ☐ HEARSAY ☐ OTHER

DESCRIPTION: _____

_____

_____

_____

_____

_____

_____

_____

_____

_____

CONCLUSION: _____

_____

_____

_____

_____

. . . AND THE WORLD IS BASICALLY GOOD.

☐ CLEAR AND COMPELLING EVIDENCE   ☐ REASONABLE DOUBT

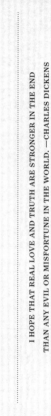

I HOPE THAT REAL LOVE AND TRUTH ARE STRONGER IN THE END
THAN ANY EVIL OR MISFORTUNE IN THE WORLD. —CHARLES DICKENS

EXHIBITS

5(a).

5(b).

EXHIBITS

5(c). _____

_____

_____

_____

_____

_____

5(d). _____

_____

_____

_____

_____

_____

EXHIBITS

5(e). _____

5(f). _____

EVIDENCE

IDENTIFICATION No. EKJR817

DATE OF COLLECTION: ___ / ___ / ___

TIME OF COLLECTION: _____ □ AM □ PM

MODE OF COLLECTION: □ OBSERVED □ OVERHEARD □ OTHER _____

LOCATION: _____

TYPE OF EVIDENCE: □ PHYSICAL □ CIRCUMSTANTIAL □ HEARSAY □ OTHER

DESCRIPTION: _____

_____

_____

_____

_____

_____

_____

§

CONCLUSION: _____

_____

_____

_____

_____

. . . AND THE WORLD IS BASICALLY GOOD.

□ CLEAR AND COMPELLING EVIDENCE □ REASONABLE DOUBT

TURNING A BAD THING INTO A GOOD THING IS UP TO YOU. —DEEPAK CHOPRA

EXHIBITS

6(a). _____

6(b). _____

EXHIBITS

6(c).

6(d).

EXHIBITS

6(e).

6(f).

EVIDENCE

IDENTIFICATION No. EKJR818

DATE OF COLLECTION: ___ / ___ / ___

TIME OF COLLECTION: _____ □ AM □ PM

MODE OF COLLECTION: □ OBSERVED □ OVERHEARD □ OTHER _____

LOCATION: _____

TYPE OF EVIDENCE: □ PHYSICAL □ CIRCUMSTANTIAL □ HEARSAY □ OTHER

DESCRIPTION: _____

_____

_____

_____

_____

_____

_____

_____

_____

CONCLUSION: _____

_____

_____

_____

. . . AND THE WORLD IS BASICALLY GOOD.

□ CLEAR AND COMPELLING EVIDENCE   □ REASONABLE DOUBT

(AFFIX OR SKETCH EVIDENCE HERE)

EXHIBITS

7(a). _____

_____

_____

_____

_____

_____

_____

_____

_____

_____

7(b). _____

_____

_____

_____

_____

_____

_____

_____

EXHIBITS

7(c). _____

_____

_____

_____

_____

_____

_____

_____

_____

7(d). _____

_____

_____

_____

_____

_____

_____

_____

EXHIBITS

7(e).

7(f).

EVIDENCE

IDENTIFICATION No. EKJR819

DATE OF COLLECTION: ____ / ____ / ____   TIME OF COLLECTION: _____ □ AM □ PM

MODE OF COLLECTION: □ OBSERVED □ OVERHEARD □ OTHER _____

LOCATION: _____

TYPE OF EVIDENCE: □ PHYSICAL □ CIRCUMSTANTIAL □ HEARSAY □ OTHER

DESCRIPTION: _____

_____

_____

_____

_____

_____

_____

CONCLUSION: _____

_____

_____

_____

_____

_____

. . . AND THE WORLD IS BASICALLY GOOD.

□ CLEAR AND COMPELLING EVIDENCE   □ REASONABLE DOUBT

(AFFIX OR SKETCH EVIDENCE HERE)

GOOD AND EVIL ARE VERY HARD TO EXPLAIN OR UNDERSTAND. —KEITH HARING

EXHIBITS

8(a).

8(b).

EXHIBITS

8(c). _____

8(d). _____

EXHIBITS

8(e). _____

_____

_____

_____

8(f). _____

_____

_____

_____

EVIDENCE

IDENTIFICATION No. EKJR820

| DATE OF COLLECTION: / / | TIME OF COLLECTION: _____ | □ AM □ PM |

MODE OF COLLECTION: □ OBSERVED □ OVERHEARD □ OTHER _____

LOCATION: _____

TYPE OF EVIDENCE: □ PHYSICAL □ CIRCUMSTANTIAL □ HEARSAY □ OTHER

DESCRIPTION: _____

_____

_____

_____

_____

_____

_____

_____

CONCLUSION: _____

_____

_____

_____

_____

. . . AND THE WORLD IS BASICALLY GOOD.

□ CLEAR AND COMPELLING EVIDENCE   □ REASONABLE DOUBT

(AFFIX OR SKETCH EVIDENCE HERE)

EXHIBITS

9(a). _____

9(b). _____

EXHIBITS

9(c). _____

9(d). _____

EXHIBITS

9(e).

9(f).

EVIDENCE

IDENTIFICATION No. EKJR821

DATE OF COLLECTION: ___ / ___ / ___

TIME OF COLLECTION: _____ □ AM □ PM

MODE OF COLLECTION: □ OBSERVED □ OVERHEARD □ OTHER _____

LOCATION: _____

TYPE OF EVIDENCE: □ PHYSICAL □ CIRCUMSTANTIAL □ HEARSAY □ OTHER

DESCRIPTION: _____

_____

_____

_____

_____

_____

_____

_____

_____

CONCLUSION: _____

_____

_____

_____

_____

. . . AND THE WORLD IS BASICALLY GOOD.

□ CLEAR AND COMPELLING EVIDENCE   □ REASONABLE DOUBT

(AFFIX OR SKETCH EVIDENCE HERE)

THE ONLY DEADLY SIN I KNOW OF IS CYNICISM. —HENRY L. STIMSON

EXHIBITS

10(a). _____

10(b). _____

EXHIBITS

10(c). _____

_____

_____

_____

_____

_____

_____

10(d). _____

_____

_____

_____

_____

_____

_____

EXHIBITS

10(e).

10(f).

EVIDENCE

IDENTIFICATION No. EKJR822

DATE OF COLLECTION: ___ / ___ / ___

TIME OF COLLECTION: _____
☐ AM
☐ PM

MODE OF COLLECTION: ☐ OBSERVED ☐ OVERHEARD ☐ OTHER _____

LOCATION: _____

TYPE OF EVIDENCE: ☐ PHYSICAL ☐ CIRCUMSTANTIAL ☐ HEARSAY ☐ OTHER

DESCRIPTION: _____

_____

_____

_____

_____

_____

_____

_____

CONCLUSION: _____

_____

_____

_____

_____

. . . AND THE WORLD IS BASICALLY GOOD.

☐ CLEAR AND COMPELLING EVIDENCE ☐ REASONABLE DOUBT

(AFFIX OR SKETCH EVIDENCE HERE)

THERE IS NO REASON WHY GOOD CANNOT TRIUMPH

AS OFTEN AS EVIL. —KURT VONNEGUT

EXHIBITS

11(a). _____

11(b). _____

EXHIBITS

11(c). _____

11(d). _____

EXHIBITS

11(e). _____

11(f). _____

EVIDENCE

IDENTIFICATION No. EKJR823

DATE OF COLLECTION: _____ / _____ / _____

TIME OF COLLECTION: _____ ☐ AM
☐ PM

MODE OF COLLECTION: ☐ OBSERVED ☐ OVERHEARD ☐ OTHER _____

LOCATION:

TYPE OF EVIDENCE: ☐ PHYSICAL ☐ CIRCUMSTANTIAL ☐ HEARSAY ☐ OTHER

DESCRIPTION:

CONCLUSION:

. . . AND THE WORLD IS BASICALLY GOOD.

☐ CLEAR AND COMPELLING EVIDENCE ☐ REASONABLE DOUBT

(AFFIX OR SKETCH EVIDENCE HERE)

TOO MUCH OF A GOOD THING CAN BE WONDERFUL. —MAE WEST

EXHIBITS

12(a). _____

12(b). _____

EXHIBITS

12(c). _____

_____

_____

_____

_____

_____

_____

12(d). _____

_____

_____

_____

_____

_____

_____

EXHIBITS

12(e). _____

_____

_____

_____

_____

_____

_____

_____

_____

12(f). _____

_____

_____

_____

_____

_____

_____

_____

EVIDENCE

IDENTIFICATION No. EKJR824

DATE OF COLLECTION: ___ / ___ / ___

TIME OF COLLECTION: _____ ☐ AM ☐ PM

MODE OF COLLECTION: ☐ OBSERVED ☐ OVERHEARD ☐ OTHER _____

LOCATION: _____

TYPE OF EVIDENCE: ☐ PHYSICAL ☐ CIRCUMSTANTIAL ☐ HEARSAY ☐ OTHER

DESCRIPTION: _____

_____

_____

_____

_____

_____

_____

_____

_____

CONCLUSION: _____

_____

_____

_____

. . . AND THE WORLD IS BASICALLY GOOD.

☐ CLEAR AND COMPELLING EVIDENCE ☐ REASONABLE DOUBT

ROSINESS IS NOT A WORSE WINDOWPANE THAN GLOOMY GRAY
WHEN VIEWING THE WORLD. —GRACE PALEY

EXHIBITS

13(a). _____

13(b). _____

EXHIBITS

13(c). _____

_____

_____

_____

_____

_____

13(d). _____

_____

_____

_____

_____

EXHIBITS

13(e). _____

13(f). _____

EVIDENCE

IDENTIFICATION No. EKJR825

DATE OF COLLECTION: ___ / ___ / ___

TIME OF COLLECTION: _____ ☐ AM ☐ PM

MODE OF COLLECTION: ☐ OBSERVED ☐ OVERHEARD ☐ OTHER _____

LOCATION: _____

TYPE OF EVIDENCE: ☐ PHYSICAL ☐ CIRCUMSTANTIAL ☐ HEARSAY ☐ OTHER

DESCRIPTION: _____

_____

_____

_____

_____

_____

_____

CONCLUSION: _____

_____

_____

. . . AND THE WORLD IS BASICALLY GOOD.

☐ CLEAR AND COMPELLING EVIDENCE   ☐ REASONABLE DOUBT

(AFFIX OR SKETCH EVIDENCE HERE)

EVERYTHING HAS BEAUTY, BUT NOT EVERYONE SEES IT. —CONFUCIUS

EXHIBITS

14(a). _____

_____

_____

_____

_____

_____

14(b). _____

_____

_____

_____

_____

EXHIBITS

14(c). _____

14(d). _____

EXHIBITS

14(e). _____

14(f). _____

EVIDENCE

IDENTIFICATION No. EKJR826

DATE OF COLLECTION: ___ / ___ / ___

TIME OF COLLECTION: _____ □ AM □ PM

MODE OF COLLECTION: □ OBSERVED □ OVERHEARD □ OTHER _____

LOCATION: _____

TYPE OF EVIDENCE: □ PHYSICAL □ CIRCUMSTANTIAL □ HEARSAY □ OTHER

DESCRIPTION: _____

_____

_____

_____

_____

_____

_____

_____

CONCLUSION: _____

_____

_____

. . . AND THE WORLD IS BASICALLY GOOD.

□ CLEAR AND COMPELLING EVIDENCE □ REASONABLE DOUBT

(AFFIX OR SKETCH EVIDENCE HERE)

EXHIBITS

15(a). _____

15(b). _____

EXHIBITS

15(c). _____

15(d). _____

EXHIBITS

15(e). _____

15(f). _____

EVIDENCE

IDENTIFICATION No. EKJR827

DATE OF COLLECTION: ____ / ____ / ____

TIME OF COLLECTION: _____ □ AM □ PM

MODE OF COLLECTION: □ OBSERVED □ OVERHEARD □ OTHER _____

LOCATION: _____

TYPE OF EVIDENCE: □ PHYSICAL □ CIRCUMSTANTIAL □ HEARSAY □ OTHER

DESCRIPTION: _____

_____

_____

_____

_____

_____

_____

_____

CONCLUSION: _____

_____

_____

_____

. . . AND THE WORLD IS BASICALLY GOOD.

□ CLEAR AND COMPELLING EVIDENCE □ REASONABLE DOUBT

EXHIBITS

16(a). _____

16(b). _____

EXHIBITS

16(c). _____

16(d). _____

EXHIBITS

16(e).

16(f).

EVIDENCE

IDENTIFICATION No. EKJR828

DATE OF COLLECTION: ___ / ___ / ___

TIME OF COLLECTION: _____ □ AM □ PM

MODE OF COLLECTION: □ OBSERVED □ OVERHEARD □ OTHER _____

LOCATION: _____

TYPE OF EVIDENCE: □ PHYSICAL □ CIRCUMSTANTIAL □ HEARSAY □ OTHER

DESCRIPTION: _____

_____

_____

_____

_____

_____

_____

_____

_____

CONCLUSION: _____

_____

_____

_____

. . . AND THE WORLD IS BASICALLY GOOD.

□ CLEAR AND COMPELLING EVIDENCE □ REASONABLE DOUBT

(AFFIX OR SKETCH EVIDENCE HERE)

IT IS IMPOSSIBLE FOR GOOD OR EVIL TO LAST FOREVER;
AND HENCE IT FOLLOWS THAT THE EVIL HAVING LASTED SO LONG,
THE GOOD MUST BE NOW NIGH AT HAND. —MIGUEL DE CERVANTES

EXHIBITS

17(a). _____

17(b). _____

EXHIBITS

17(c). _____

17(d). _____

EXHIBITS

17(e). _____

17(f). _____

EVIDENCE

IDENTIFICATION No. EKJR829

DATE OF COLLECTION: ___ / ___ / ___

TIME OF COLLECTION: _____ ☐ AM ☐ PM

MODE OF COLLECTION: ☐ OBSERVED ☐ OVERHEARD ☐ OTHER _____

LOCATION: _____

TYPE OF EVIDENCE: ☐ PHYSICAL ☐ CIRCUMSTANTIAL ☐ HEARSAY ☐ OTHER

DESCRIPTION: _____
_____
_____
_____
_____
_____
_____
_____
_____
_____
_____

CONCLUSION: _____
_____
_____
_____
. . . AND THE WORLD IS BASICALLY GOOD.

☐ CLEAR AND COMPELLING EVIDENCE ☐ REASONABLE DOUBT

THE SUN IS ALWAYS SHINING. WE HAVE OXYGEN, TREES, BIRDS. THERE'S SO MUCH GOOD THINGS ON EARTH, STILL. WE HAVEN'T DESTROYED EVERYTHING. —ZIGGY MARLEY

EXHIBITS

18(a). _____

18(b). _____

EXHIBITS

18(c). _____

18(d). _____

EXHIBITS

18(e). _____

18(f). _____

EVIDENCE

IDENTIFICATION No. EKJR830

DATE OF COLLECTION: ___ / ___ / ___

TIME OF COLLECTION: _____ □ AM □ PM

MODE OF COLLECTION: □ OBSERVED □ OVERHEARD □ OTHER _____

LOCATION: _____

TYPE OF EVIDENCE: □ PHYSICAL □ CIRCUMSTANTIAL □ HEARSAY □ OTHER

DESCRIPTION: _____

_____

_____

_____

_____

_____

_____

_____

_____

_____

_____

CONCLUSION: _____

_____

_____

_____

. . . AND THE WORLD IS BASICALLY GOOD.

□ CLEAR AND COMPELLING EVIDENCE   □ REASONABLE DOUBT

(AFFIX OR SKETCH EVIDENCE HERE)

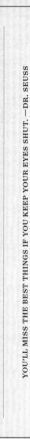

YOU'LL MISS THE BEST THINGS IF YOU KEEP YOUR EYES SHUT. —DR. SEUSS

EXHIBITS

19(a). _____

19(b). _____

EXHIBITS

19(c).

19(d).

EXHIBITS

19(e). _____

_____

_____

_____

_____

_____

_____

_____

_____

_____

19(f). _____

_____

_____

_____

_____

_____

_____

EVIDENCE

IDENTIFICATION No. EKJR831

DATE OF COLLECTION: _____ / _____ / _____

TIME OF COLLECTION: _____
☐ AM
☐ PM

MODE OF COLLECTION: ☐ OBSERVED ☐ OVERHEARD ☐ OTHER _____

LOCATION: _____

TYPE OF EVIDENCE: ☐ PHYSICAL ☐ CIRCUMSTANTIAL ☐ HEARSAY ☐ OTHER

DESCRIPTION: _____

_____

_____

_____

_____

_____

_____

_____

§

_____

CONCLUSION: _____

_____

_____

_____

. . . AND THE WORLD IS BASICALLY GOOD.

☐ CLEAR AND COMPELLING EVIDENCE   ☐ REASONABLE DOUBT

(AFFIX OR SKETCH EVIDENCE HERE)

I BELIEVE THAT MAN WILL NOT MERELY ENDURE; HE WILL PREVAIL. —WILLIAM FAULKNER

EXHIBITS

20(a). _____

20(b). _____

EXHIBITS

20(c). _____

20(d). _____

EXHIBITS

20(e). _____

20(f). _____

EVIDENCE

IDENTIFICATION No. EKJR832

DATE OF COLLECTION: ___/___/___   TIME OF COLLECTION: _____ □ AM □ PM

MODE OF COLLECTION: □ OBSERVED □ OVERHEARD □ OTHER _____

LOCATION: _____

TYPE OF EVIDENCE: □ PHYSICAL □ CIRCUMSTANTIAL □ HEARSAY □ OTHER

DESCRIPTION: _____

_____

_____

_____

_____

_____

_____

_____

CONCLUSION: _____

_____

_____

. . . AND THE WORLD IS BASICALLY GOOD.

□ CLEAR AND COMPELLING EVIDENCE   □ REASONABLE DOUBT

(AFFIX OR SKETCH EVIDENCE HERE)

THERE IS NOTHING EITHER GOOD OR BAD

BUT THINKING MAKES IT SO. —WILLIAM SHAKESPEARE

EXHIBITS

21(a).

21(b).

EXHIBITS

21(c). _____

21(d). _____

EXHIBITS

21(e). _____

21(f). _____

Created and published by Knock Knock
1635-B Electric Ave.
Venice, CA 90291
knockknockstuff.com

ISBN: 978-1-60106716-6
UPC: 825703-50205-3